DEVON TORS
a family pottery

VIRGINIA BRISCO

© Virginia Brisco 1998

Published by Virginia & Bill Brisco, Inglefield
218 Sandridge Road, St. Albans, Herts. AL1 4AL

ISBN 0 9520045 1 8

CONTENTS

WILLIAM SAMUEL BOND	5
FORMATION OF THE DEVON TORS ART POTTERY	13
THE WORKFORCE	17
Sam Shufflebotham	21
Joseph Nekola	23
Arthur Steer	23
Arthur Bowden	24
Arthur Rowley	24
PRODUCTION IN THE 1920's AND 30's	26
THE WAR YEARS	38
THE POST WAR YEARS	40
THE END OF THE POTTERY	45
THE BOND FAMILY TREE	46
HOW TO IDENTIFY DEVON TORS POTTERY	49

Plate I *Top left: Vase with lizard handles, 10" (25 cms) tall. c. 1930. Top right: Jug 7" (17.5 cms) tall, moulded with flowers and leaves in relief; copied from a Staffordshire jug, 1930's. Bottom left: Vase 9" (23 cms) tall, red clay which has been covered in white slip and carved to expose the red body; decorated with "Bacchante dancing" and "Phrygian lady" on reverse. Decorated by Elizabeth Grimaldi 1960. Bottom right: Another vase by Elizabeth Grimaldi; this one is $10\frac{1}{4}$" (26 cms) tall, incised decoration and applied slips, 1950's.*

INTRODUCTION

This is the story of the Bond family who, for four generations, were potters in South Devon, mainly in Bovey Tracey. Great Grandfather William Samuel Bond was attracted into pottery at the Bovey Pottery Company as it expanded to meet the needs of a rapidly growing working class. His sons also learnt the trade but they decided to start their own pottery, the Devon Tors Pottery, making hand crafted wares for the tourist trade as well as some high quality art pottery. Sadly, this pottery closed in the late 1960's although its wares are sought by many ceramic enthusiasts and pottery collectors. The story of the Bond family of potters is fascinating in its own right, but it is also a microcosm of a once flourishing South Devon industry that has now all but disappeared.

WILLIAM SAMUEL BOND - Master Potter

In the nineteenth century the ceramics industry was changing rapidly; the old country potters, who for centuries had supplied local needs, were being superceded by the big factories. The advances of the Industrial Revolution meant that domestic china could be mass produced cheaply, and the improvement in transport enabled these goods to be sent all over the country. Most of the 'factory potteries' were in Staffordshire but there were other pockets of production, one of these being Bovey Tracey. The Bovey Tracey potteries were established in the mid-eighteenth century and made some highquality earthenware, but by the mid-nineteenth century they were superceded by the Bovey Tracey Pottery Company (under John Divett) which was expanding rapidly to meet the growing demand for mass produced items. The pottery became the largest employer in Bovey Tracey with well over 160 employees, many attracted by the higher wages than they could earn in agriculture or other rural trades; William Samuel Bond was one such person.

Fig. 2: *Left to right: Frank Bond, William Bond (seated), and John Bond. Photo taken in 1913, most probably on the occasion of their father's funeral.*

Map to show the location of the Devon Tors Art Pottery

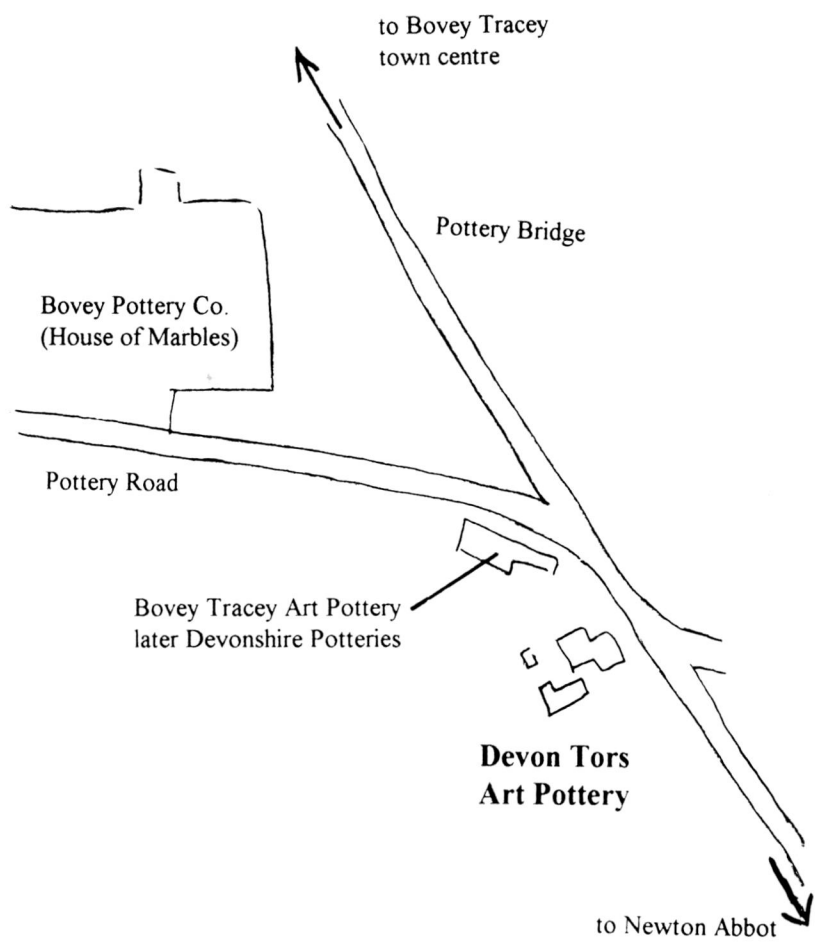

William Samuel Bond was born in 1858, the son of William Bond, an agricultural labourer of Fore Street, Bovey Tracey. William Samuel went into the pottery, possibly encouraged by his older step-siblings, Sarah and Henry Steer, who already worked there. Having gained some basic training at the Bovey Pottery Company, he decided to broaden his experience by going to Staffordshire with a couple of other lads. The 1881 Census Returns record William Samuel Bond, a potters plate maker, and his two friends, William Maple (also a potters plate maker) and David Parks (potters handler) boarding at the home of William Bennett at 37 Park Street, Stoke-on-Trent. William Bennett was a potters dish maker and his wife Amelia a potters paintress; they were both 75 years old and were also looking after their grandson Joseph who was only four years old but already a 'scholar'.

There was a considerable interchange of potters between Staffordshire and Devon - the Staffordshire potters were attracted by the cleaner air and milder climate in Devon, whilst the Devonians were attracted by higher wages and a desire to see the world-famous potteries of Stoke-on-Trent.

Whether William Samuel Bond grew tired of the smoke and grime of 'The Potteries' or whether it was the charms of a lady may never be known but towards the end of 1881 he returned to Bovey Tracey and married a local girl, Bessie Snell, at the Baptist Chapel. The newly-weds set up home in Heathfield Terrace and their first son, William George, was born the following year.

By the 1870's there were developments afoot in South Devon which were to affect both the potting industry in that area and the Bond family. In 1869 Mr. G. J. Allen of Watcombe House, St. Marychurch, established a terracotta works to exploit the fine quality clay he had discovered on his land a few years previously. Mr. Allen's motives were to create high quality works of art and to do this he recruited skilled potters from Staffordshire who would teach their craft to local people and provide additional employment. The Watcombe Pottery achieved wide acclaim for the quality of its wares and could count amongst its customers none other than Queen Victoria,

members of the royal families in Britain and Europe, as well as many of the aristocracy who liked to over-winter in the milder climate of the Torquay area.

A decade later at Newton Abbot another philanthropic local gentleman, John Phillips, was establishing his own art pottery to provide both employment and artistic education. John Phillips was a fervent exponent of the Arts and Crafts Movement and adopted its philosophy both at his pottery, known as the Aller Vale Art Pottery, and in the Cottage Art Schools which he helped to run.

Although the output of the Watcombe Pottery and the Aller Vale Pottery were initially very different, they both represent aspects of the Art Pottery movement. This was a reaction against mass production and inhuman working conditions in favour of a return to hand made pottery produced in small establishments where individualism was encouraged and valued. Although the initial high motives were modified (mainly through economic necessity) the individual hand made approach led to the establishment of over twenty potteries in the South Devon area, including the Devon Tors Pottery. However, that is to jump ahead by thirty years!

In 1885 Mr. John Divett died and this was to cause great uncertainty regarding the future of Bovey Tracey Pottery Company. His sisters and cousin attempted to carry on the company but business suffered and by 1894 it was on the verge of closure. It was rescued in 1895 and a new company, Bovey Pottery Co. Ltd. was created. It was the uncertainties following Divett's death that probably prompted William Samuel Bond to seek work at the Watcombe Pottery - the family moved to St. Marychurch in the late 1880's. William's brother-in-law Jack Snell was already working at Watcombe; the Bond family has a tile he made in 1879 - it is moulded in

Fig. 3: *Top: Devon Tors pottery in the 1920's. Bottom: The workers c. 1936. Left to right, back row: Joseph Nekola (decorator), G. Carpenter (decorator), Arthur Steer (thrower), Ken Bond (glaze dipper and kiln setter), S. Short (slip dipper), E. Wyatt (caster), Robert Fry (plate Maker). Bottom row: Arthur Bowden (decorator), Frank Bond (jollier). Bill Bond (mould maker), Sam Shufflebotham (decorator), S. Potter (kiln fireman).*

relief with a classical style female figure playing a tambourine. By this time both Jack and William were highly skilled master potters and could turn their hands to any aspect of the trade - mould making, decorating and throwing on the wheel. The family also has a plaque which William decorated and dated 1893 - it is painted with a blue tit amongst foliage and flowers with a border of apple blossom; another moulded vase has apple blossom painted on to unglazed terracotta, typical of Watcombe's production in the 1890's.

The Bonds lived at 5 Pettitwell Cottages, St. Marychurch, and while they were there two more sons were born, Frank in 1891 followed by John Charles in 1895.

Sometime around the turn of the century the Bonds returned to Bovey Tracey and William went back to his old firm, now renamed Bovey Pottery Company Ltd., which was now a thriving pottery again. His sons William George and Frank also joined the pottery when they left school and their father was keen for them to follow in his footsteps and become master potters. However, all was not well for William Samuel as he was suffering from silicosis, a regrettably common condition amongst potters, and died in 1913 - he was 54 years old. His youngest son was only 18 years old and seeing the effects of silicosis perhaps explains why he chose *not* to go into the pottery trades. William George was now married to Ella Fletcher (a potters daughter) and they were expecting their first baby, a boy whom they called William Stanley (Stan).

During the first two decades of the twentieth century the "famous Devonshire pottery" began to attract wide attention due to the popularity of mottowares. These were pots which were hand thrown from local red clay, dipped in cream slip, decorated with a simple design and a motto or saying which

Plate II *Top row: Selection of toby and face jugs from the 1930's; the largest 'Uncle Tom Cobleigh' is $7\frac{1}{2}$" (19 cms) tall and has a musical box under the shoulder. Middle row: Two Art Deco style vases (larger one is 6" tall) and a double dish decorated by Sam Shufflebotham, 1930's. Bottom row: Vases and a jug from the 1930's - 40's. The tallest vase is $5\frac{3}{4}$" tall and is decorated with a thrush moulded in relief.*

was scratched through the slip. The public loved the mottoes and the addition of a place-name to the pots made them very popular tourist souvenirs, an appropriate gift for the workers to take home from their day out at the seaside, or from that new invention, the Annual Holiday.

World War I stunted demand and production but once the war was over demand increased again with a seemingly ever expanding market. Many potters decided to set up on their own and this led to a proliferation of small potteries all over South Devon - the Devon Tors Art Pottery was one of these.

FORMATION OF THE DEVON TORS ART POTTERY

William George (Bill) and Frank Bond both saw active service in the Great War and after their return they decided to start their own pottery. Together with their friend, Robert Fry, they acquired premises on the Newton Road, not far from Bovey Pottery Co. Ltd., and the Devon Tors Art Pottery opened in 1921 (see map). Bill and Frank Bond did the potting whilst Robert Fry was an 'administrator' - the Kelly's Directories in the 1920's and 30's refer to him as 'secretary'.

The pottery buildings were very primitive and consisted of a few wooden huts, as can be seen in the photos (fig. 3). Joyce Harfield is the daughter of John Bond, brother to Bill and Frank; in the 1930's - 40's she visited the pottery every year; here she recalls memories of the pottery in the 1930's when she was still a child:

The main hut was long and narrow, with a sink 8 to 10 feet long at one end. This was where the clay was washed and pummelled by hand. The men were covered in a bright pink powder, as the red clay, splashed on to them, dried out. I don't think it ever washed out of their clothing, or aprons and shoes. Some would change their shoes to go home, but even these held the tell-tale powder on their soles.

Fig. 4: Top left: Frank Bond on the left and Arthur Rowley; top right: Arthur Steer; Bottom left: Cynthia Bond; bottom right: Stan Bond.

The inside walls of this hut were lined with benches, interspersed with potters wheels. These were propelled by hand, and foot. Above were countless brackets which took the planks holding unfinished products, drying out before their biscuit firing, or biscuit ware awaiting decoration or glazing. Moulds for making toby jugs, Dartmoor pixies, cup and jug handles, etc., were stored below the benches.

Down the centre of this long workshop were even more shelves, all stacked with pieces of ware in differing stages of completion. Young men would carry them on to the next processing stage. Even on the outside the walls were covered with brackets on to which loaded planks could be set down. Beyond the workshop stood the packing shed. Partitioned shelves along the sides held the sorted orders. Bales of straw and boxes covered the floor. Untreated clay was stored on the ground behind the packing shed in an open-sided area covered only by a roof.

Two further buildings were constructed in the 1930's. These were used as Decorating and Glaze dipping shops. Between them were two bottle kilns, the ovens like deep cupboards with arched ceilings. I loved to walk into them when they were emptied but still warm and to watch them being filled with ware to be fired, each piece stacked so that no one pot touched another. A work of art. When full, the entrance to the oven would be bricked up, except for small spy holes, and sealed with clay. The kilns were coal-fired and, once lit, would burn continuously night and day until the clay thimbles, visible through the spy-holes, turned over from the top, indicating the correct temperature had been reached. I can recall being lifted up to look through these holes, and into the white hot ovens.

The kilns Joyce describes were 4 hole coal fired kilns; they took 65-70 hours to fire and used 3 tons of coal per firing.

Some further improvements were carried out after the Second World War, in particular to update the showrooms. Joyce describes the scene when visitors came:

Fig. 5: *Top: Frank Bond turning; bottom: Ken Bond packing the kiln.*

Visitors were always welcomed and during the summer months charabancs would arrive with parties two or three times a week. In later years, particularly on wet days, the forecourt would be filled with coaches. There was always a lot of laughter and fun when visitors were there, and quite a few sales.

However, the pottery buildings remained very basic. Cynthia Quick (nee Bond) recalled that when she worked at the pottery in the 1950's and 60's it was freezing cold in the winter and her hands were swollen with chilblains; there were no proper 'facilities' and the only toilet was on an 'Elsan' out the back!

In spite of these conditions the potters and other workers seemed to have enjoyed working there and their pots bear testament to their skills and pride in their work.

THE WORKFORCE

Devon Tors was very much a family business, employing three generations of Bonds. Bill and Frank were the mainstay during the interwar years, with Frank's son Ken joining the pottery in the mid 1930's. Bill's son, William Stanley (Stan) joined them after World War II and Stan's daughter Cynthia went to the pottery when she left school in 1958 and stayed there about ten years - by this time she was married and expecting her first baby. Bill really loved the pottery and even after he had retired he still came in - he especially loved chatting to visitors.

Bill and Frank Bond could turn their hands to many pottery crafts but perhaps Bill's greatest skill was as a decorator. He was very confident in his brushwork and could execute superb

Plate III *Top left: Powder box in the form of a cottage, $5\frac{1}{2}$" (14 cms) tall overall, decorated by Joseph Nekola for Ken Bond's wife, Joyce, in 1939. Top right: Goose, decorated by Nekola in the late 1930's, jug in the shape of a chick, 1950's. Bottom left: Negro head trinket box, $4\frac{1}{2}$", ($11\frac{1}{2}$ cms) tall, early 1950's. Bottom right: Moulded dogs - the one on the left is made of red clay, and is 7" (18 cms) tall, smaller one in white clay. 1930's - 50's.*

scrolls. One of his other specialities was the Widecombe Fair series and he was responsible for all those until he retired when his grand-daughter Cynthia took over.

Frank Bond did most of the jollying work, and Stan did maintenance (he was a carpenter) and general work. Ken was a glaze dipper and kiln setter - he recalled that when his Uncle Bill worked part time for Bovey Pottery Company he often used to bring buckets of glaze to Devon Tors at 6.00 a.m. - they had come "out of the back door". Bovey Pottery Co. Ltd. used top quality clear glazes.

Cynthia inherited her grandfather's skills as a decorator and did most of the design work and 'specials' in the late 1950's and 60's; it was her idea to paint little daisies on the backs of models of Bambi and the public loved them. Cynthia also did scrollwork, some of the cottages, and little dishes with a crinoline lady in the middle. Cynthia used to have to go to the showroom if visitors came in - even now she can remember all the prices:
"Bambis" were 3/3 (16 pence) each, big geese 2/6 (12p) each, small geese 1/6 each, or a set of one big and two small for 5/6 (27p)".
One of the most expensive items in the showroom was the one pint tankard decorated with all the Widecombe characters - it sold at one guinea (£1.05). If only we could find them at those prices today!

In addition to the family, Devon Tors employed a variety of other workers on a full-time, part-time, or casual basis. Such were the uncertainties of potting in the 1920's and 30's that even the Bond brothers and Robert Fry had to find work at Bovey Pottery Co. Ltd. on a part-time basis just to survive; they would work two or three days a week at 'Big Bovey' (as it was known) and the rest of the time at Devon Tors. This

Fig. 6: *Photo taken during World War II. Left to right: Bob Fry, Jan Plichta (agent), Arthur Steer, Monica Doyle (the first woman to work at Devon Tors), Bill Bond and Frank Bond. Bottom: The workers c. 1968, left to right: Ken Bond (tucked at the back), Colin Maunder, Bill Bond, Cynthia Quick (nee Bond), Stan Bond, Arthur Rowley, Bert Gilding, Frank Bond and Arthur Steer.*

flexible approach enabled Devon Tors to survive the Depression of the early 1930's when several other local potteries, such as Daison Art Pottery in Torquay, went into liquidation.

The photographs in figs. 3 and 6 show some of the people who worked for Devon Tors. Many of them were skilled craftsmen and some, such as Joseph Nekola and Sam Shufflebotham were highly skilled decorators whose work is eagerly sought by collectors today. The story of some of these characters is recorded here.

Sam Shufflebotham

Samuel Walter Shufflebotham, known as 'Shuff', was at Devon Tors from c. 1935 to the end of 1939. Ken Bond remembers him well and describes him as "a queer old stick who used to shuffle along as he was bad on his feet". Shuff lived in Torquay and used to come out to Bovey Tracey on the bus. Sam Shufflebotham came initially from Staffordshire (and never lost his accent), he was employed at Pountneys in Bristol until about 1908 when he went to Llanelli Pottery for about seven years before returning to Pountneys. He went to Torquay about 1930 and remained there until his death in 1940 at the age of 64.

Shuff specialised in designs of flowers (roses were a favourite), fruit, cocks and hens, and Dutch figures. His work at Pountneys and Llanelli is highly sought by collectors, but his work at Devon Tors has been neglected, probably because so little is known about it. The photos of the showroom taken c. 1935 (fig. 7) include decorations of fruit which are undoubtedly Shuff's work because of their similarity to his designs at the earlier potteries. The colour picture (Plate II) of a dark green double dish decorated in black with apples is also one of Shuff's designs. He also painted Violet's bottles, seagull and kingfisher patterns whilst at Devon Tors. Sam Shufflebotham is

Fig. 7: *Two photos of the showroom in the 1930's. The fruit decoration was a new line by Sam Shufflebotham.*

also believed to have worked at Bovey Pottery Co. Ltd., Barton Pottery and the Torquay Pottery Co. during his time in South Devon.

Joseph Nekola

Joseph Nekola was the son of Karel Nekola and he came to Bovey Tracey c. 1930 when their Wemyss factory in Scotland closed down. Their designs were made at Bovey Pottery Co. Ltd. and many of these are very 'collectable' today as 'Bovey-Wemyss' - they are usually stamped 'Plichta' the name of the agent. What is not so widely known is that Joseph Nekola also worked at Devon Tors, often painting identical designs, as can be seen in the goose in Plate III - the shape is identical to Plichta, the only difference being that Devon Tors used red clay. The powder box in the style of a cottage also shown in Plate III was painted by Nekola for Ken Bond's wife - it is inscribed "Joyce, April 1939".

Arthur Steer

Arthur Steer was an expert thrower and taught throwing at evening classes at the Art School - quite an achievement for someone who left school at the age of 9 and was never literate. He started potting at Torquay Pottery Company and came to Devon Tors when it started. Joyce Harfield has recalled her memories of watching Arthur Steer at work in the 1930's:

Plate IV *Top row: Advertising items: teapot depicting Peartree cafe at Ashburton; Cider jug 6" (15 cms) tall inscribed 'Here Meda Cider is made, Meadhay, Dunsford, Devon'; mug decorated with the Commercial Inn at Bishopsteignton. Middle row: Small toby jug inscribed 'The Ferns, Xmas 1939'; teapot made to commemorate the Golden Wedding of Mr. & Mrs. Bert Gilding in 1960 - Bert Gilding worked at Devon Tors; small bowl made for the May Day Bazaar organised by Totnes Divisional Labour Party in 1926; vase, inscribed on the reverse "with the Devonport Petty Officers Best wishes for 1932". Bottom Row: Selection of items made in the 1950's and 60's; many were designed by Cynthia Bond. The jam pot on the right has the "odd spot" version of polka dots.*

"I loved being lifted up on to a high bench to watch Mr. Steer at work on the potters wheel. In his odd moments he would amuse and delight me by making ever changing shapes. He would pretend to lose control of the clay, to screw it up, then start again. It was magic".

Arthur Steer continued to work for Devon Tors up until the time it closed in the late 1960's; he and Ken Bond then moved to Aidees, who had purchased Devon Tors.

Arthur Bowden

Arthur Bowden was a decorator and worked at Devon Tors from the 1930's to the 1960's (with a break during the war). He did all the 'specials' such as the commissioned mugs depicting inns, or the Pear Tree Cafe teapot (Plate IV). Arthur painted the Devon Tors toby jugs, especially the large ones which required more skilled work; he was a very competent artist and also had a studio in Chudleigh where he sold paintings.

Arthur Rowley

Arthur Rowley was an engineer and electrician at the local lignite pits but he also helped out at Devon Tors from time to time. The mug decorated with a view of Bovey mill (fig. 8) is initialled 'AR' on the base indicating it was made by Arthur Rowley - the inscription is rather poorly written, evidence of his lack of potting skills. Arthur loved talking to visitors and sometimes talked for an hour at a time - if he was lucky he got a few tips! However, the company were not always pleased

Fig. 8: *Top left: Mug, 4¾" (11 cms) tall, decorated with a flying mallard above bulrushes and inscribed "VHG" on the reverse (a personalised commemorative). Inside the mug is a model of a frog, shown in the photo below. Top right: Mug with sgraffito and slip decoration of Bovey Mill - decorated by Arthur Rowley and initialled by him on the base. Bottom right: Black mug with white slip scrolls and 'icing' inscription 'The Taw River Inn'. All from the 1950's. Note the typical Devon Tors handles.*

because if the visitors were kept talking for too long they would usually leave the pottery instead of going to the showroom to buy a few pots to take home.

A few other workers also warrant mentioning. John Heywood was a fireman - he had worked at Lemon and Crute in Torquay before he came to Devon Tors; he fired his last kiln there at the age of 85. Vincent Kane was a modeller who had worked for Bovey Tracey Art Potteries, subsidiary of Torquay Pottery Company; when it closed in 1946 he went to Devon Tors and worked there for six years. One of the 'outworkers' employed by Devon Tors in the 1950's and 60's was Elizabeth Grimaldi, who was then in her 70's (at least!); some of her work can be seen in Plate I. Miss Grimaldi, an Italian, lived at Exeter and she would collect vases in their biscuit state (i.e. after their first firing), take them home where she carved and painted them, then returned the pots to Devon Tors for glazing and firing. Her work is exquisite and must have been done as a real 'labour of love'.

PRODUCTION IN THE 1920's AND 30's

Devon Tors was established to benefit from the growing popularity of what is known as 'Torquay pottery' (then known as Devonshire pottery). This was mainly slip decorated mottowares and pigment or slip painted kingfishers, etc., on a blue ground. So, not surprisingly, most of their early production concentrated on these wares. Devon Tors produced its own version of cottagewares and the scandy pattern (Plate V and fig. 10); although their cottages are very much in the style of Torquay versions made at Watcombe they have their own individuality too. Devon Tors cottages are usually squat

Fig. 9: *Top row: Teapot, cup and jug with sgraffito 'sketches' of the Widecombe Fair characters. Middle row: left to right: Gift ware of Devon violets (perfume from Aidees) in an egg cup in a presentation box; jug, $2\frac{3}{4}''$ (7 cms) tall, decorated with violets and inscribed 'To Mother', 1930's; violets scent bottle, 1930's. Bottom Row: Selection of scent 'bottles'; the one second from the left is a candleholder and would have held a glass phial of scent.*

with deeply overhanging roofs (to represent thatch) and there are often two or three birds in the sky. But their most distinguishing feature is the blue, used for borders as well as the main decoration, which they called lapis lazuli - it is a vivid vibrant blue which none of the other potteries could emulate. The same blue is found on the scandy pattern. In addition to the standard scandy, Devon Tors did their own variation with pink and buff centre 'fronds' and a 'foot' of scrolls at the bottom (Plate V).

Examples of Devon Tors Kingfishers are shown in Plate V. The birds are moulded in relief and they are usually well decorated and perched amongst foliage over water and lilies. Another version depicted two kingfishers facing each other with a waterfall in the background - possibly meant to represent Becky Falls, or maybe any other waterfalls in the Dartmoor area.

Other popular items for tourists were scent bottles, filled with Devon violets or some other perfume, and almost all the Torquay potteries made them. Some of the Devon Tors examples are shown in fig. 9 - the pixie sitting on a mushroom was exclusive to them although Bovey Pottery Co. Ltd. made a similar version in white clay. A novelty scent bottle was shaped like a candlestick and would take a phial of scent - the same items were also sold as part of dressing table sets. Although Devon violets were the most popular scent bottles, Devon Tors also made some with Welsh lilac, and lavender for Cussons. Devon Tors scent bottles are frequently stamped with a capital B on the base.

As Devon Tors became more widely known so they felt confident enough to try new and original lines. The most popular was undoubtedly the Widecombe Fair characters sgraffitoed on to a wide range of items such as teapots (fig. 9), mugs, tankards, cups and saucers, bowls, egg cups, condiment

Fig. 10: *Top left: The reverse of the scandy jug shown on the front cover; top right: jug, 8¼" (21 cms) tall with sgraffito drawing of Buckfast Abbey; bottom left, typical Devon Tors Cottageware from the 1930's; bottom right: humorous 'cartoon' of the steps at Clovelly with a donkey looking towards one of the new 'Belisha beacons' with a 30 m.p.h. speed limit! 1934.*

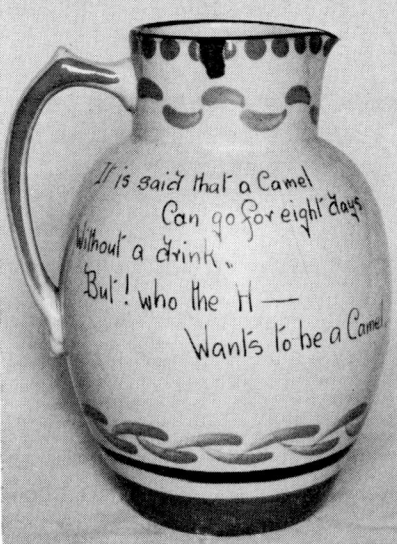

sets. The red clay pots were dipped in buff coloured slip (a creamy mixture of clay and water) and when dry the design would be incised to show the red body - the technique is called sgraffito. Joyce Harfield describes the process:

"The decorating I most enjoyed was sgraffito, where the design or motto was scratched out with a needle. Characters, such as Uncle Tom Cobley, were pricked out on to tracing paper which would be placed on the ware and dusted with chalk, or charcoal dust. The dust would penetrate through the pin pricks, transferring the design on to the article to be sgraffito'd!"

At Devon Tors the etching was done with their own 'tool', made by attaching a gramophone needle to a piece of wood. Widecombe Fair items are believed to have all been done by Bill Bond until his retirement in the 1960's when his grand-daughter Cynthia took over. The pots sometimes had a head of one of the characters, or larger items might have all the characters including the Old Grey Mare. A pint tankard has been seen with the horse standing amongst grass which has been applied using the 'mocha' technique - this was probably a 'one-off'. Large consignments of Widecombe ware were sold by the Middleweeks who had (and still have) shops at Widecombe in the Moor; some of these carried a backstamp 'Widecombe Pottery'.

With the popularity of Widecombe ware, the sgraffito technique was adapted for other decorations. 'Sketches' of tourist attractions were often used e.g. the jug with Buckfast Abbey shown in fig. 10, a jug depicting Lorna Doone Farm, Malmshead, the mug with the water mill at Bovey Tracey (fig. 8), or the tankard depicting the Steps at Clovelly with a donkey and the inscription "Come on Belisha" - Belisha beacons were first introduced in 1934 to serve as warnings to motorists, so that must date this tankard fairly accurately!

Plate V *Top row: Cottagewares and the scandy pattern. Middle row: Kingfisher patterns - the birds are moulded in relief. Bottom row: A selection of animals; the squirrel is $5\frac{1}{2}$ (14 cms) tall. The donkey on the right was made from a Plichta mould*

Another popular fashion of the 1920's and 30's was to have teapots, jugs, condiment sets, and a whole range of domestic items made in the shape of thatched cottages (Plate VI). many factories produced them, although amongst the Torquay potteries only Devon Tors and Torquay Pottery Company appear to have done so. Collectors often get confused when trying to identify unmarked examples, although with a little experience it is easy to tell the difference. Devon Tors cottages have a wide dark green band of 'grass' around the base, and lapis lazuli delphiniums (or hollyhocks) around the cottage walls. Whilst Devon Tors used rectangular shaped cottages for cheese dishes and powder bowls, they never appear to have done so for jugs, teapots, sugar bowls, etc. So a round cottage jug or teapot (made of brown clay) is almost certainly Devon Tors, a rectangular one is almost certainly Torquay Pottery Company or its subsidiary Bovey Tracey Art Pottery.

Toby and face jugs were another range of items which Devon Tors marketed. The initial mould for the toby jug was made from a Staffordshire example, and both the Staffordshire toby and its Devon Tors copy are shown in Plate VII. The Devon Tors toby is smaller due to the shrinkage of the clay during firing. This toby has a hat and was intended as a tobacco jar, the majority were made as jugs - a selection is shown in Plate II. The largest face jug has a deep 'collar' which housed a music box which played the Widecombe Fair tune; it is inscribed "Uncle Tom Cobley" (or Cobleigh, both spellings were used). These type of face jugs were only made in the late 1920's and early 1930's whereas tobies were made right through to the post war period. Toby jugs were made in several sizes, some were made as lamp bases, and they came with a wide variety of different coloured coats.

Fig. 11: *Top left: Small jam pot decorated by Bill Bond with scrolls done in blue pigments, 1930's; top right: cigarette box in the form of a drum to advertise The Drum Inn at Cockington, early 1930's; middle row, left: small mug $2\frac{1}{2}$" (6.5 cms) tall, decorated with violets and inscribed British Legion, Chudleigh, 1934'; right: teapot stand with cameo style decoration, 1930's; Bottom left, shaving mug, $3\frac{1}{4}$" (8 cms) tall, plain yellow, late 1940's. Bottom right: Small shallow bowl decorated by Cynthia Bond, early 1960's.*

Models of animals were popular lines in the showroom and were bought by adults and children alike; some are shown in Plates III and IV. Making a model required considerable skill because it then had to be used to make a mould from Plaster of Paris. Some master moulds would be cast, and these were called Blocks, which could be used to make many more Plaster of Paris moulds for slip casting. Plate VII shows a Block and mould for a dog and Plate III shows the finished dogs. Plaster of Paris moulds wear out after a few dozen casts are made. Almost all Devon Tors animals were made from red clay, although some of the smaller versions of the dog were cast in white clay. Other animals made in the 1930's include squirrels, penguins (in at least two sizes) rabbits in several sizes and geese in at least two sizes. Little models of pixies sitting on a hump (about 2" tall) were made in their hundreds, if not thousands, they were a cheap and cheerful souvenir which reminded the holiday-makers of the little pixies they had hoped to see up in the moors!

With the fashion for Art Deco styles in bright colours, Devon Tors introduced their own versions, and adapted other shapes to suit the new craze. Plate II shows two vases with strips, or 'splodges' of bright colours. Another popular line was a monocoloured bulbous vase with a deep neck which had geometric shaped 'wings' applied to the shoulder of the vase. Plate VI shows two multi-coloured pots which were also made in the 1930's, although in more muted shades than the Art Deco range. The swirling effect was achieved by mixing coloured slips in a special funnel which Bill and Frank Bond's brother John (Jack) had made - he borrowed some welding equipment from the gas works just along the road. Even though John did not work at Devon Tors he was a frequent visitor and was prepared to 'help out' if he could.

Fig. 12: *Top left: Plate, 6¼" (16 cms) diameter decorated in pigments with a black Spitfire and deep pink border. Inscribed on the reverse 'Made and decorated by Robert G. Fry 1942'. Top right: Plate 8½" (21 cms) diameter, decorated with a fish on a black ground. Decorated by 'Chris', a young art student from Lustleigh. Bottom left: Teapot, 7" (18 cms) tall overall, in the form of a round cottage and inscribed 'NAHS" 1935'. Made for the Newton Abbot Hospital Saturday Carnival, most probably as a prize. Bottom right: Model of a snail, 6" (15 cms) wide overall, blue with white 'oddspot' pattern. 1950's.*

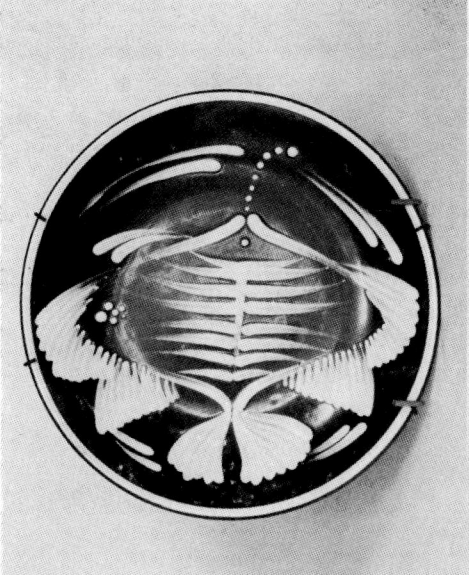

Devon Tors was a small pottery making all the pots by hand so it was ideally suited for tackling small commissions or even individual pots for special occasions. Plate IV shows a selection of these. Some items were made as advertising wares such as the teapot depicting Pear Tree Cafe at Ashburton, or the jug painted with a view of Dunsford and advertising Meda Cider - it is inscribed 'Here Meda Cider is made, Meadhay, Dunsford, Devon', A vase with a pigment painted windmill is inscribed 'With the Devonport Petty officers best wishes for 1932', presumably given as a Christmas or New Year gift. A small mug, decorated with violets (a standard line) became a commemorative when inscribed 'British Legion, Chudleigh, 1934' (fig 11). Ken Bond has said that his father and uncle were very generous to local causes, and one example can be seen in fig. 12. this teapot is inscribed 'NAHS 1935' and was given as a prize for one of the events in 'Newton Abbot Hospital Saturday', an annual carnival to raise funds for the local hospital - it is a very rare commemorative.

Many of the 'specials' were decorated by Arthur Bowden such as the Sun of Canada Cricket Club souvenir for their annual Devon Tour. Their secretary would go into the pottery at the start of the week armed with a photo of their host's cricket pavilion and the names of all players (about 15 or 16). Arthur Bowden would then reproduce the pavilion on the mugs, in sgraffito and slip, and inscribe each one with the name of a player; these delightful souvenirs would be glazed, fired, and ready to take home by the end of the week. The pavilions that have been seen are Newton Abbot for the 1937 tour, and Exmouth for 1938.

One commemorative that didn't come to fruition was Devon Tors' plan to make a terracotta bust of Edward VIII for his abdication (see Plate VIII). However, Devon Tors could not get official permission to do these so only a few were made "illegally". They have a white 'icing' inscription on the back which says "As we knew him". Pub mugs were a speciality of

Plate VI *Top row: Two jugs with swirling slip decoration; the ribbed neck of the jug on the right is often found on Devon Tors items. Bottom row: Biscuit barrel and cheese dish in the form of cottages. 1930's.*

Devon Tors and most of these were decorated by Arthur Bowden (Plate IV) - they are highly sought by collectors today. Those that have been seen include the Sloop Inn at St. Ives, the Three Pilchards Inn at Polperro, the Foxhunters Inn near Ilfracombe, and the Old Commercial Inn at Bishopsteignton. This last mug was sold at the pub, and many are inscribed on the reverse 'North, South, East or West, Bill Moles is the Best', a reference to Bill Mole, landlord of the Old Commercial Inn from the 1920's to c. 1955 when he died. The mugs sold for 2/6 ($12\frac{1}{2}$p) each.

Occasionally the potters at Devon Tors were able to use their skills to make individual pieces, and two of these are shown in Plate I. The vase with lizards is $14\frac{3}{4}$" tall and is a magnificent example of the potters art; it dates from c. 1930. Only two or three other examples have been seen, including a smaller version entirely in blue, so they are very rare. Even rarer is the jug moulded and decorated with flowers and leaves. It is one of a set of three jugs, the tallest being 7", and they were copied from Staffordshire originals. The set is owned by a member of the Bond family and is the only one the author has seen - yet, as they are moulded, more must have been made. Collectors should look out for them!

Devon Tors also offered visitors the opportunity to decorate their own pots which would then be glazed and fired ready for collection a week or so later. These were often very different in style to the usual Devon Tors products although they would be in the Devon Tors range of colours. Collectors finding such "oddities" should be aware of these possible origins, especially if pieces are signed.

THE WAR YEARS

World War II had a devastating effect on many potteries because of a shortage of labour as men were called up, difficulty in getting materials, and government restrictions which, from 1942, prohibited the use of coloured decoration for all wares intended for the home market. The Bovey Tracey Art Pottery, a subsidiary of Torquay Pottery Co., which was almost

Fig. 13: *A school party visits the pottery in the early 1960's.*

next door to Devon Tors closed completely and was used as a flour store. Devon Tors, though, managed to survive the disruption and upheaval. Joyce Harfield describes how one problem was overcome:

"*During the Second World War the Red clay was difficult to acquire. My uncles would go to the road works in and about the Torquay area to see if any clay had been excavated. If it had they would 'test' its consistency in their mouths to check if it was suitable for their purpose and, in this way, they managed to keep going*".

The workforce was depleted to five in all, but now included a woman, Monica Doyle, the first woman to be employed by Devon Tors (see fig. 6). Most of the pots that were sold were undecorated and the bulk were sold to Jan Plichta - these were plates, cups and saucers, etc., which were brown clay with white slip inside the cups. Many hundreds of plain terracotta pitchers were made in several sizes up to 14 pints. Devon Tors also adapted a pint mug by cutting away the side to make a "blackout light" (Plate VIII).

In spite of restrictions a few decorated items were made, probably 'illegally', and one of these is shown in fig. 12. The plate, $6\frac{1}{4}$" in diameter, is decorated with a Spitfire and is inscribed "Never was so much owed by so many to so few", a quotation from Winston Churchill's speech to the House of Commons on 20th August 1940 in praise of R.A.F. pilots during the Battle of Britain. On the back of the plate is written 'Made and decorated by Robert G. Fry 1942' - Robert Fry was not a decorator although he may have done this for himself or a friend. A mug has also been seen with the same decoration.

THE POST WAR YEARS

After the war was over the government was slow to remove restrictions in the belief that this would enable the economy to recover faster - all restrictions on the potteries were not removed until 1952 and then only under pressure from ceramics manufacturers who wanted to make coronation souvenirs. However, by this time there was a shortage of labour and wages were rising which forced prices up and made the pottery expensive. All the South Devon potteries felt the effects of this and began to 'cut corners' to compete with cheaper mass produced wares.

Devon Tors continued with many of its old lines, such as mottowares, but simplified them, e.g. there were fewer blue dots round the rims of cottagewares and the scandy pattern was gradually dropped as it took longer to execute. Tobies, scent bottles and animals continued to be made, although often with fewer colours. Many toby jugs and other souvenir ware was sold from a kiosk in Buckfast Abbey car park by a man called Will Young - these items had 'Buckfast' on the base. Will Young was a potter himself and modelled some lively little character figures of the Widecombe Fair men which he fired in a small backyard kiln at his home.

The popular models of geese continued to be made although Cynthia Quick (nee Bond) has said that when she joined the pottery they stopped wiping the slip off the wings of the geese; although this only took a second or two, on a day's production

Fig. 14: *Bill Bond decorating Widecombe ware, 1956. Towards the back of the bench are a row of negro head trinket boxes.*

it would make a significant difference to costs. Some new models were added to the animal range, such as the snail shown in fig. 12 and a jug in the form of a chicken (Plate III). When Bovey Pottery Company Ltd. closed Devon Tors managed to acquire some of the animal moulds that were 'lying around' and then produced their own versions - the donkey shown in Plate V was one of these and also a model of two rabbits sitting 'cheek to cheek'.

The Bonds were quick to seize any opportunities to cut costs. In the mid 1950's a pub was being built opposite Longpark Potteries in Torquay and the clay that was dug out was free to anyone who wanted to collect it; Devon Tors took away 90 tons.

Many new lines were introduced, the polka dot and white scrolls on coloured grounds being the most popular. Ken Bond says that the polka dot pattern was inspired by a lady who visited the pottery wearing a dress in this pattern. Coincidentally, the Watcombe Pottery in St. Marychurch also claim the same origin for their polka dot pattern, but Watcombe's 'lady in a polka dot dress' was said to be Princess Margaret! There is no evidence that Princess Margaret visited Watcombe. In any case, as polka dots were fashionable, no doubt lots of ladies went into lots of potteries wearing polka dot dresses! Devon Tors used white polka dots on a variety of backgrounds - brown, lime green, royal blue, black, and these same background colours were also used for the scroll pattern which comprised a band of scrolls around the middle of pots. A variation of the polka dot pattern consisted of larger dots of more irregular size - this was called 'Oddspot' (Plate IV). The standard polka dot pattern was cheaper to produce because it could be done by less skilled paintresses, whereas it was a highly skilled job to ensure that the scrolls were evenly spaced round the pot. Bill Bond did many scroll decorations. Egg cups decorated with scrolls cost 2/6 ($12\frac{1}{2}$p) each, the same as the cottage pattern, whereas polka dots were only 1/6 ($7\frac{1}{2}$p) each.

'Contemporary' colours of lime green, yellow, turquoise, royal blue and orange were very popular in the 1950's and 60's and Devon Tors brought out a wide range of decorations in these

Plate VII *Top: Staffordshire toby tobacco jar on the left and the Devon Tors copy on the right. Bottom: Block and mould for making slip cast models of dogs; the lines on the block denote cutting lines for the mould.*

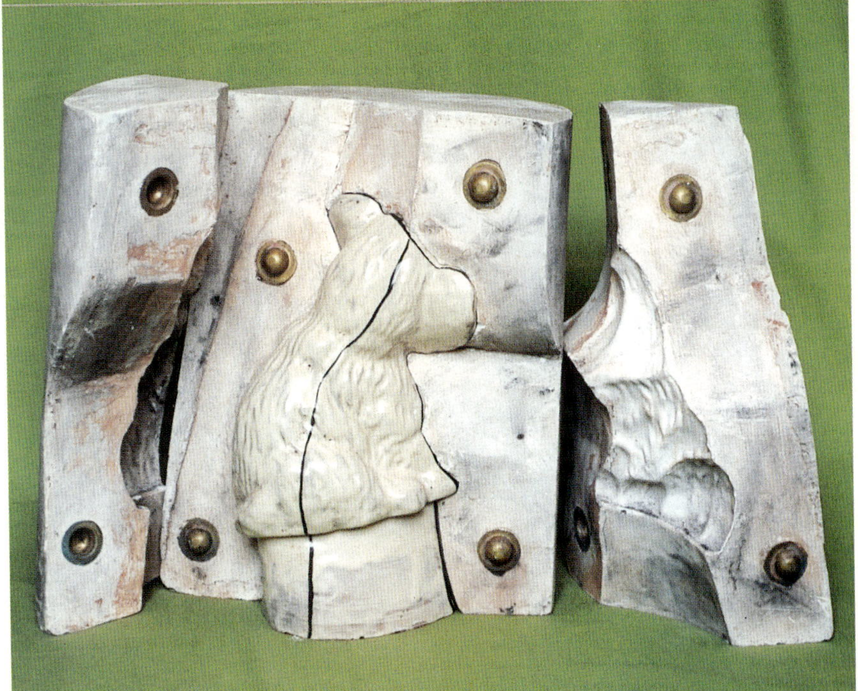

colours - Plate IV shows some of these; many of the designs were originated by Cynthia Bond. In many cases old shapes were brought up to date simply by using new colours, as with the shiny black pixie on a mound (Plate VIII) which first appeared in the 1930's in green.

Devon Tors also brought out a range of plates with highly stylised depictions of animals' such as cockerels, a crab and a fish (see fig. 12). The plates were either black with white or very pale blue paintings, or else pale blue plates with black decoration. Ken Bond recalled that many were done by a young art student called Chris who worked for Devon Tors during his summer vacation from college, although Ken cannot remember his surname. 'Chris' lived with his parents in Lustleigh. Cynthia Bond also decorated plates in a similar style, usually cockerels, and she painted a matched pair of plates for herself - they are believed to be the only pair that were made, all the others were facing the same way (to the right).

Novelties were popular with the public too, and the mug shown in fig. 8 is an example of this. The mug is decorated with a flying mallard, but when the imbiber has come to the end of his drink he will be face to face with a frog, attached to the inside of the mug. No doubt it caused much amusement. Little models of pixies sitting on a mound had been introduced in the 1930's but remained popular throughout the post war period - the visitors and holiday makers bought them for Good Luck.

In the 1950's 'negroes' were all the rage - heads, busts, models, dolls, etc.; this was part of a general increase in interest in African art and culture which grew as a consequence of decolonisation. Devon Tors produced a negro head trinket box - see Plate III. Cynthia Quick recalled that the trinket boxes were known as 'black boys' even though they are quite obviously girls! The example which is illustrated has a pink and green decorated headscarf and collar, others were in blue and white 'odd spot'; some were also made with much paler faces to represent gypsies.

THE END OF THE POTTERY

In spite of the cost cutting at Devon Tors it became increasingly difficult to keep the business profitable. Visitors declined as more people took holidays abroad and hand crafted pottery was no longer so fashionable. With great reluctance, in 1967, Ken Bond decided to sell the business; of the original potters, Bill Bond had died in 1964 and Frank was in his 70's and well past retirement age. The business was sold to the 'next door neighbours', Aidees, who made novelty wares, perfume pots, etc.; Ken Bond and Arthur Steer went to work at Aidees too. There was still a lot of pottery at Devon Tors in the process of production and Ken took this to a firm at Newton Abbot for firing and it was then sold off. Aidees soon demolished the buildings and that was the end of the Devon Tors Art Pottery.

Within three years Frank and Stan had died leaving Ken and Cynthia as the only surviving family potters. However, what has survived are the products of the Devon Tors Art Pottery - some functional domestic wares, some novelties and animals, and some beautiful works of art - testimony to the skills of a family of potters.

THE BOND FAMILY TREE

Names shown in bold type worked in the potteries

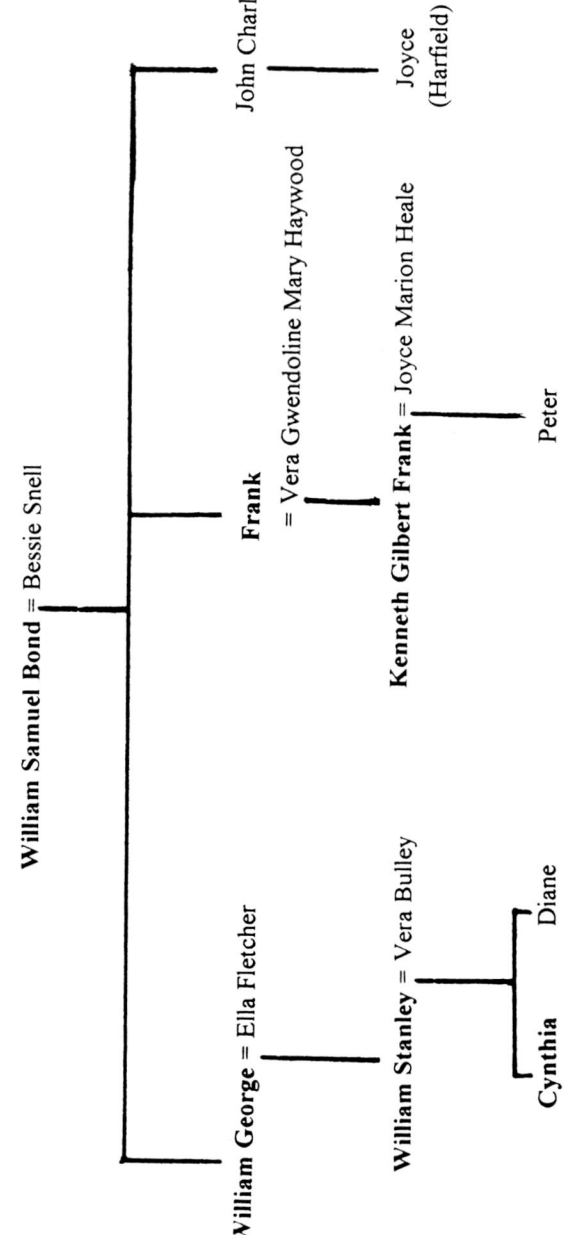

THE BOND FAMILY TREE

William Samuel Bond (1858-1913) was the son of William and Harriet Bond. In 1881 he married Bessie Snell, the daughter of George Bowden and Ellen Snell, and they had three sons: William George, born 1882; Frank, born 1891; and John Charles, born 1895.

William George (Bill) Bond (1882-1964) married Ella Fletcher, the daughter of James Fletcher, potter; they had a son, William Stanley.

Frank Bond (1891-1971) married Vera Gwendoline Mary Heywood and they had a son Kenneth Gilbert Frank.

John Charles Bond married Beatrice Esther Batten and they had a daughter Joyce, who married Bertie Harfield. John was a plumber by trade and did not work at the pottery.

William Stanley (Stan) Bond (1913-70) married Vera Bulley and they had two daughters, Cynthia and Diane.

Kenneth Gilbert Frank (Ken) Bond (b. 1921) married Joyce Marion Heale and had a son, Peter.

Cynthia Bond (b. 1943) married Barry Quick.

DEVON TORS POTTERY — Impressed 1921-1960's

 Black rubber stamp 1930's-1960's

 Black rubber stamp

B — Impressed

DEVON TORS ART POTTERY BOVEY TRACEY — Incised

Incised or white 'icing' inscription Sold by Will Young

Buckfast

Widecombe Pottery — Incised or white 'icing' inscription Sold by Middleweeks

HOW TO IDENTIFY DEVON TORS POTTERY

Devon Tors had a policy of backstamping everything sold in their showroom but items sold to other outlets were normally unmarked, or else had the name of the retailer on the base. Known marks are shown opposite. In the absence of a backstamp there are some clues to identification:-

- brown clay was normally used, although a few very late items in particular animals, were made in white clay

- the base was either dry or glazed. Dry bases were more common in the 1920's and 30's. Glazed bases have a tendency to look 'greasy'

- look at the colour used for decoration; the lapis lazuli is a very distinctive shade of blue, not found on any other Torquay mottowares

- look at the shapes of handles, the handles shown in fig. 8 were exclusive to Devon Tors.

DEVON TORS MOTTOES

Most Devon Tors mottowares have short sgraffitoed sayings and place names, although some larger items may carry longer mottoes. A giant sized globular shaped teapot, decorated with cottages, has been seen with a very amusing verse, which is reproduced here - spelling as on the pot:

> *Give me a mind that is not bored*
> *That does not whimper, whine or sigh*
> *Don't let me worry over much*
> *About that little thing called I*
> *Give me a sence of humor Lord*
> *Give me the grace to see a joke*
> *To get some happeness from life*
> *And pass it on to other folk.*

DEVON TORS ART POTTERY Co.

Makers of High-class
DEVON WARE

VISIT THE EX-SERVICE POTTERS AT WORK

Motorists and Visitors Invited
Conducted Inspection of Works
FREE CAR PARK

NEWTON ROAD, BOVEY TRACEY
Buses stop at Pottery

Advertisement from the 1938 edition of the Devon General Bus Company's timetable.

Plate VIII Top left: Model of a pixie on a mound, 5" (12.5 cms) tall 1950's. Top right: Model of a cat, $6\frac{1}{2}$" (16.5 cms) tall, 1950's. Bottom left: Terracotta bust of Edward VIII $6\frac{1}{2}$" (16.5) cms) tall - white 'icing' inscription of the back "As we knew him" - these never went into production as Devon Tors was refused a licence for manufacture. Bottom right: Pint mug converted into a Blackout light during World War II.

ACKNOWLEDGEMENTS

The inspiration for this book was an article written by Joyce Harfield for the Torquay Pottery Collectors Society magazine of October 1991; this kindled my interest in Devon Tors and I subsequently visited Joyce and Bert Harfield to talk about the pottery. Joyce put me in touch with her cousins, Ken Bond, and Cynthia Quick (nee Bond). I was able to visit them all on several occasions. I am most grateful to Joyce, Ken and Cynthia for all their time and patience in talking to me about Devon Tors and in showing me their pottery, photos, etc. I hope I have done them justice in this book.

I should also like to thank Sydney Reed and Joyce Stonelake for allowing me to photograph pots from their collections.